This Notebook Belongs To:

____

____

____

Enjoying this Notebook?

Please leave a review because we would love to hear your feedback, opinions and advice to create better products and services for you! Also, we want to know how you creatively use your notebooks and journals.

Thanks for your support!
You are greatly appreciated!

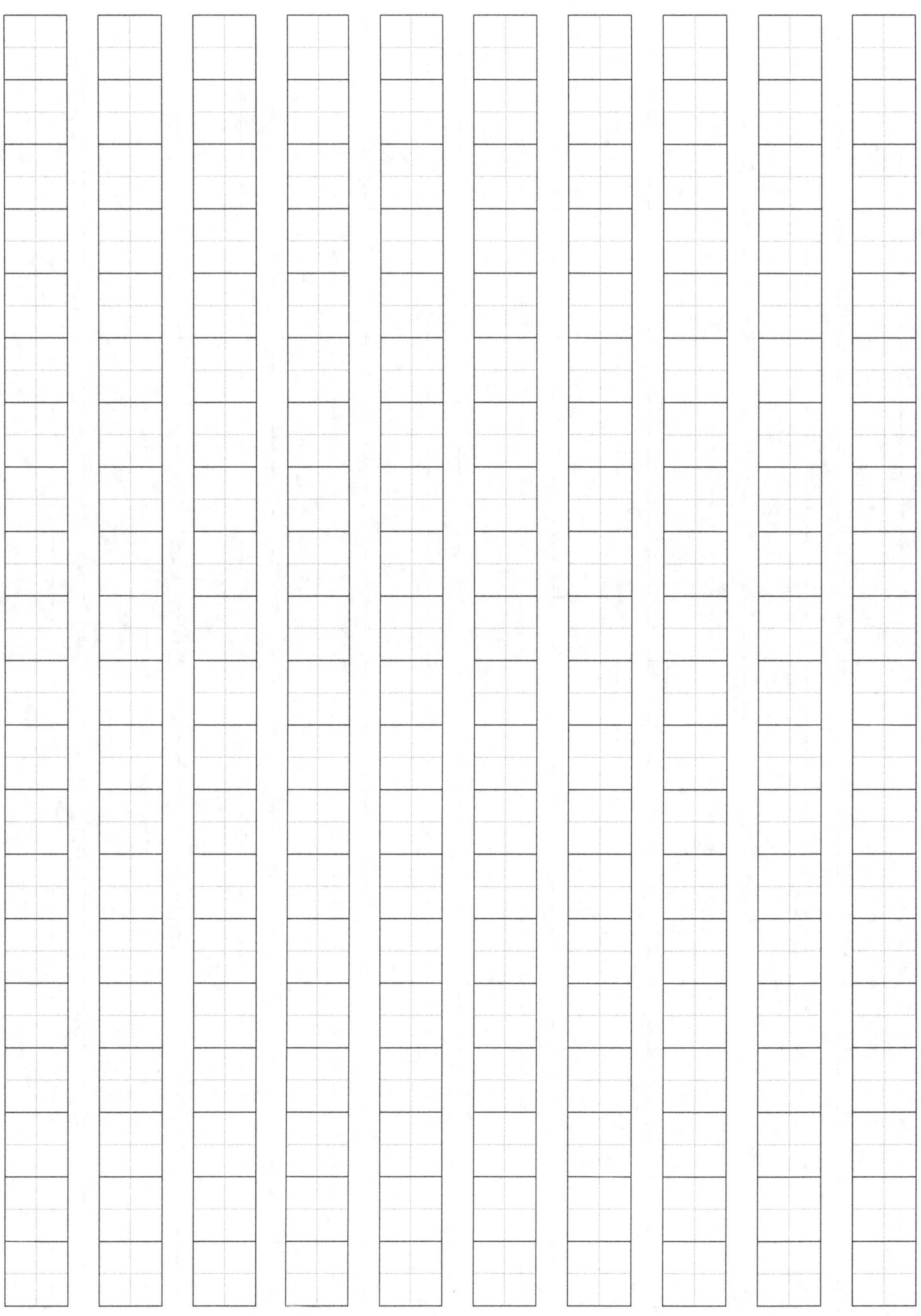

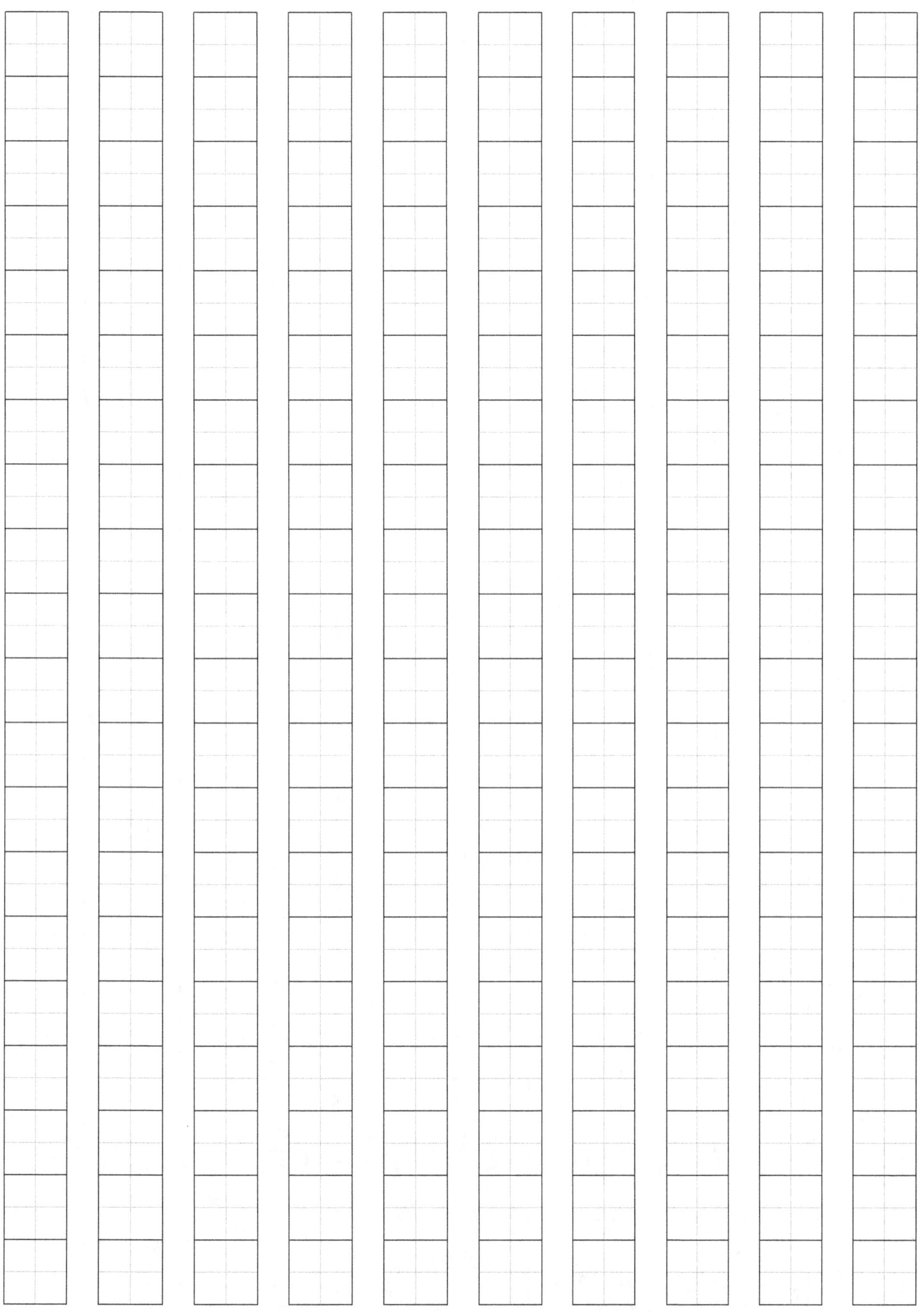

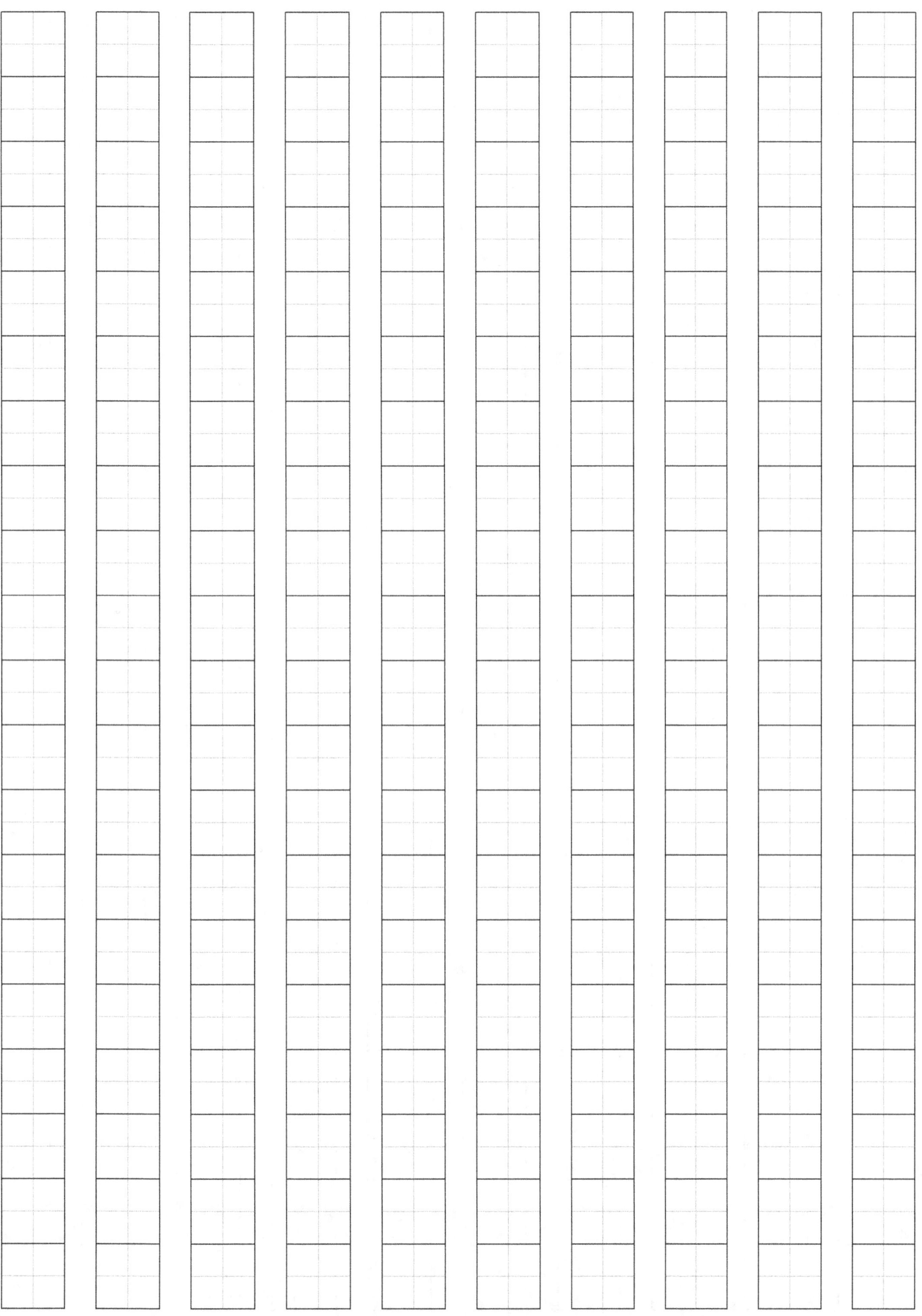

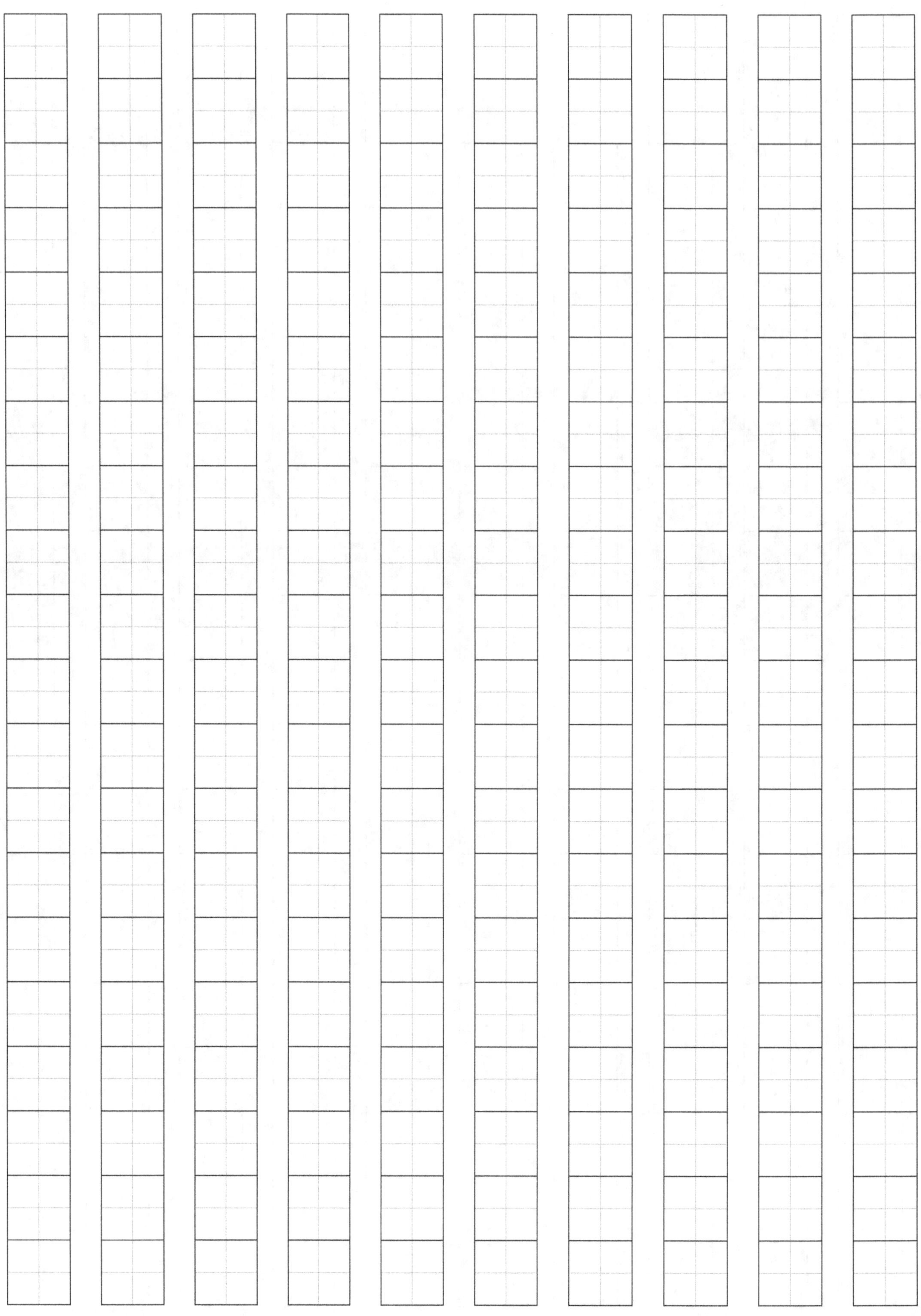

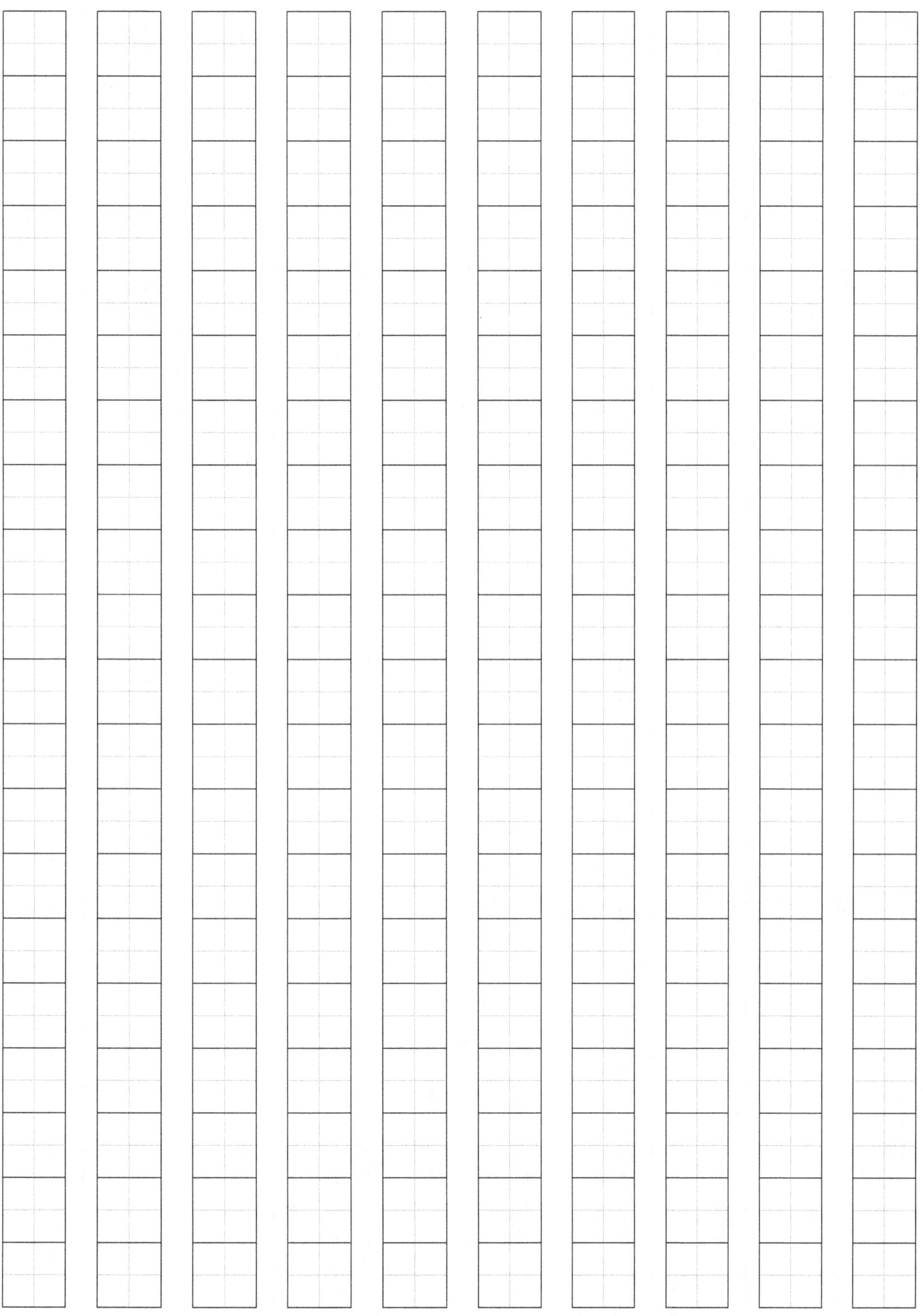

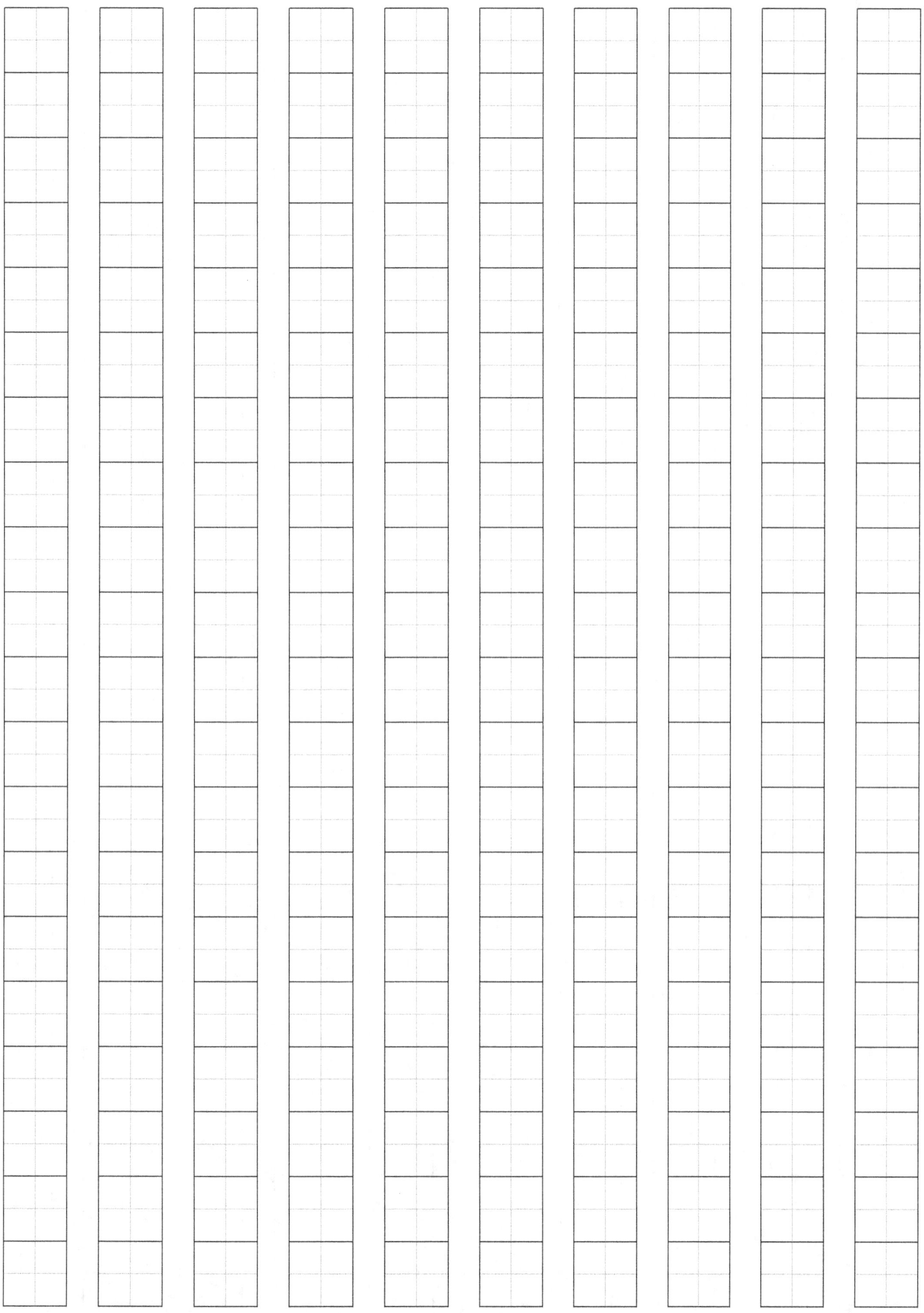